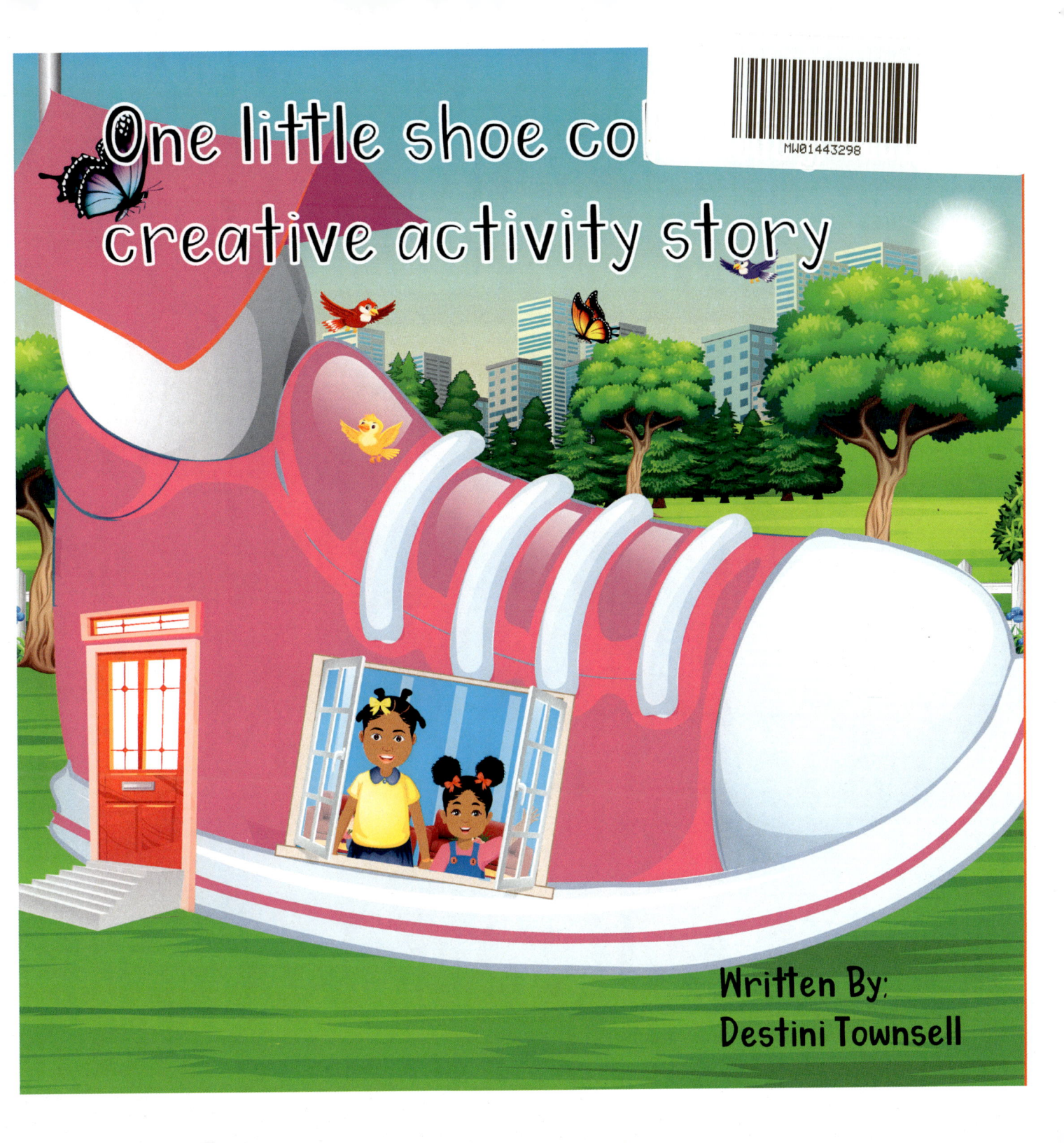

One little shoe colorful creative activity story

Written By:
Destini Townsell

If I walked in my sister's shoes, I wouldn't be able to walk at all!

Mom just brought her home, and all she does is crawl.

She is always in my way.

eating up all my snacks,always wanting me to play

Mom, when is this Lil girl going home?

She's always in my face.

Jumping on my bed.

Oh My God(OMG) not my new game Did she just break one ? no freaking way!

Playing in the park

Ivy hurry up let's go , we have to get home and get ready for School

Ivy's 1st day of school

Mom
MOM MOM is IVy ready it's her first day .

It's going to be so much fun and so much to learn and do .

We can jump in muddy puddles, play in the sand, eat ice cream, and do our favorite dance

Ivy how was your first of school

Omg it was so cool ,everybody wanted to be my friend ,and play with me ,we learned our ABC's and 123's

We even made slime, Slime can you believe it slime. It was so fun I think I love school.

Mom, I guess I'm kind of happy I have a Little sister, so I can teach her everything.

How to be strong and powerful and a little silly too.

maybe it's not so bad

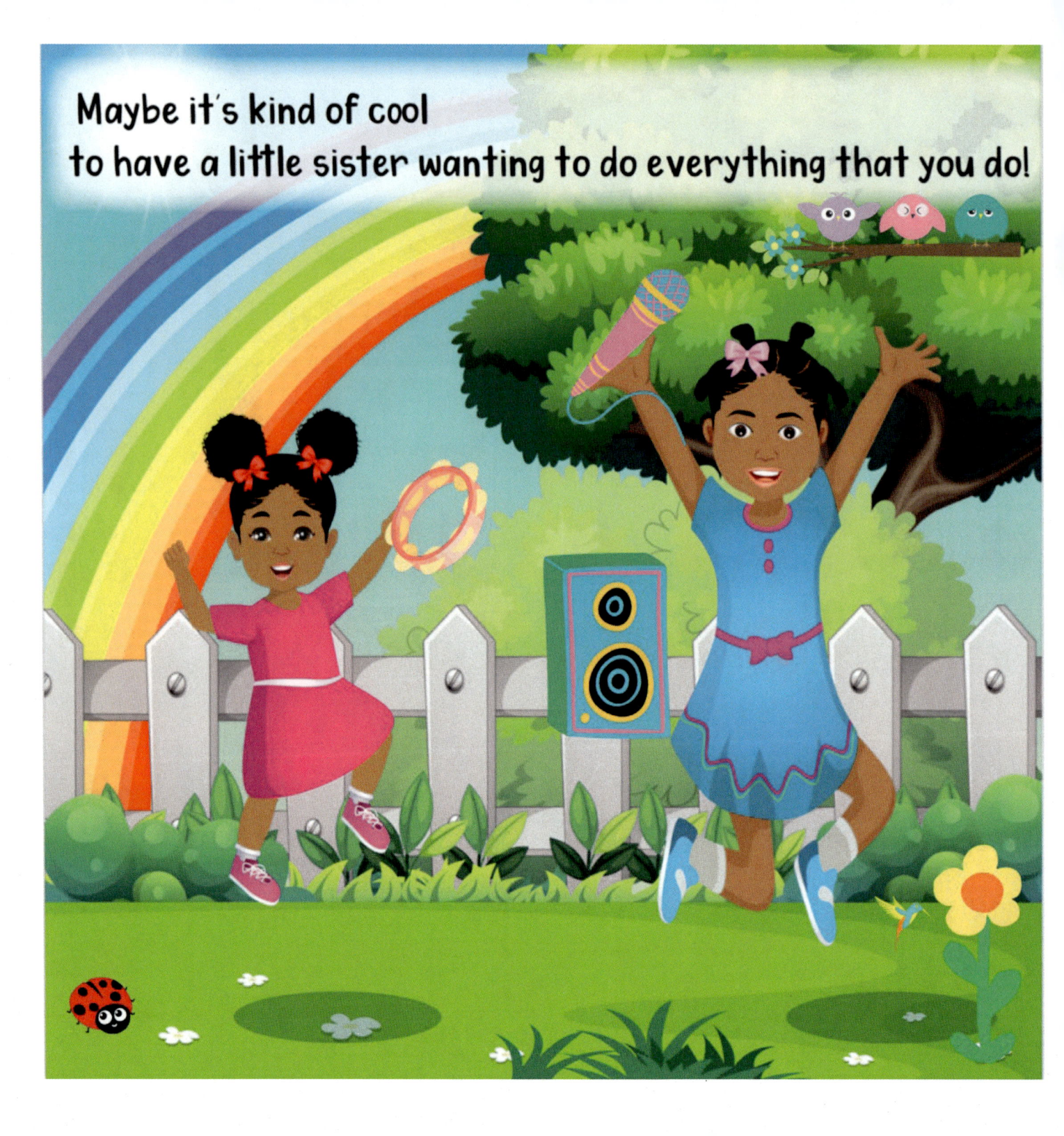

Maybe it's kind of cool
to have a little sister wanting to do everything that you do!

FUN BANG!

COLORING AND CREATIVE ACTIVITY PAGEs

DO NOT MISS OUT ON THE FUN

nyiahsandisfunsuppliesss

It's Niah's & I's Fun Supplies

Written By:
Destini Townsell

CONNECT THE DOTS

Niah's & I's Fun supplies

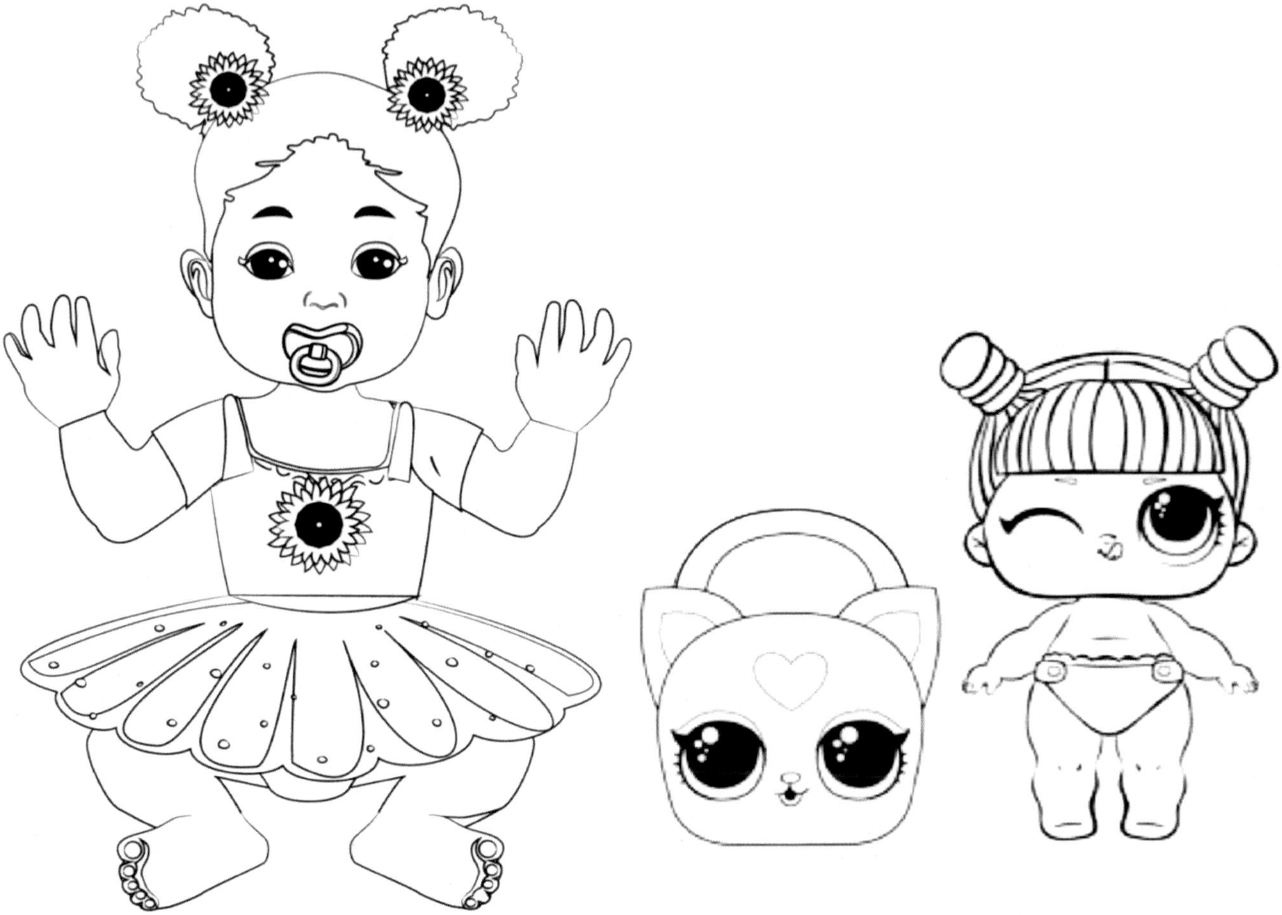

BOSS
BOSS
MAMA
BOSS

fun in the sun honey

Help Nyiah find her little sister

S	U	R	P	R	I	S	E
D	M	B	F	Q	L	G	C
O	C	F	U	N	O	V	I
L	H	A	K	X	L	Z	W
L	G	E	J	S	Y	C	H
B	I	R	T	H	D	A	Y
W	N	U	V	O	S	K	F
R	O	K	P	B	A	E	Z

thank you for buzzing

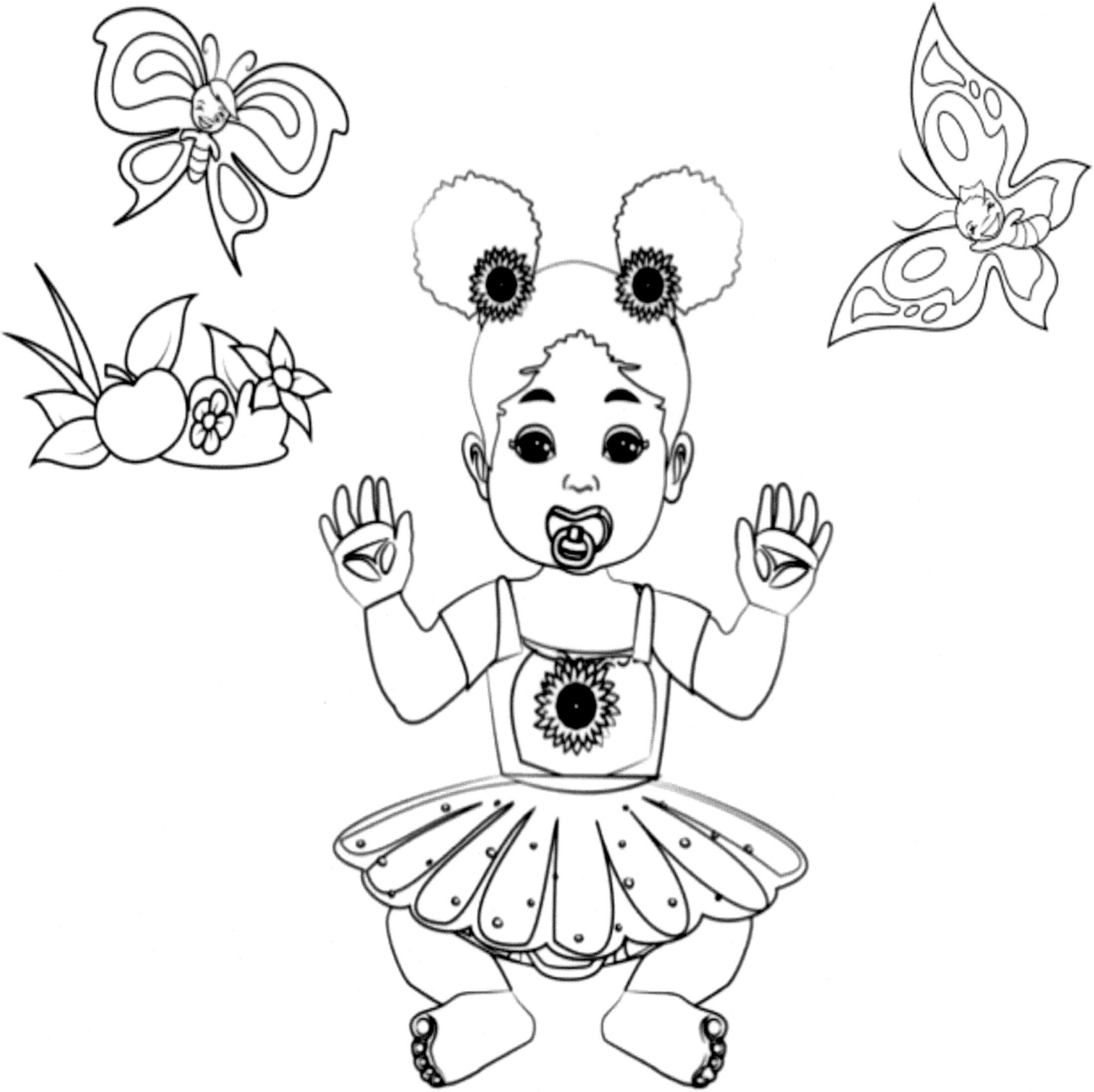

One Little Shoe coloring and activity story

SMILES N° FROWNS ™

I am important and you are two , we are sister let's stick together and take over the world and do what we do!

-um

Yum! I Like Gum!

Yum! I like gum!
I like to chew gum.
I like to chew gum and hum.
My mum has gum.
She gives me some.
Yum! Yum!
I like to chew gum!

1. I like _____.
○ plums
○ gum
○ buns

2. I like to chew and _____.
○ run
○ play
○ hum

3. She gives me _____.
○ some
○ plums
○ jam

4. Who has gum?
_____
_____
_____

Pinky Splash CHEW TM.

REAL SPLASH

100% PURE SPLASH

FRESH PRODUCT   350 ml

Ingredients:
BubbleGum made with Koolaid

- 2 teaspoons Koolaid powder (drink crystals)
- 1 tablespoon lily white corn syrup/organic honey
- 3 tablespoons gum base h
- 1/2-1 cups icing sugar aka - Powdered sugar

Procedure:
1. Combine gum base, corn syrup, and flavoring in a microwavable bowl. Stir together then heat in the microwave for 30 seconds to soften the gum base.
2. Stir mixture together, and then heat for another 30 seconds.
3. Once mixture has liquefied, pour it on to a well of icing sugar on a non-stick mat. It will be hot! Gently fold it into the icing sugar using a small spatula. Once it has cooled enough to the touch, continue to knead the gum into the icing sugar as stickiness requires.
4. Once gum piece is smooth and no longer sticky, tear or cut gum into bite sized pieces and store in a ziplock container for 1-2 weeks.

Best Before: 23/02/2025

NIAH'S AND I'S FUN SLIME

How to create!

Instructions

Add three cups of white shaving cream (not clear shaving cream) to a large mixing bowl. ...

Add 1/2 cup Elmer's School Glue to the mixing bowl.

Add a teaspoon of baking soda to the mixing bowl.

Stir everything together with a spatula or large spoon.

Add a tablespoon of contact solution (15 ml) to the bowl.

:camera: nyiahsandisfunsuppliesss

NIAH'S AND I'S PIZZZA TIME

Start a garden in your backyard
A Kids' Gardening Idea for Pizza Lovers

Kids love pizza, so let the older ones help you divide a garden area into "pizza slices." Encourage them to plant tomatoes, peppers, onions, spinach and other kid-friendly pizza foods.

After the veggies are ready to pick, let older children help you slice or chop them for the pizza. Little ones can spread tomato sauce on the dough, arrange the vegetables on the dough and top the pizza with shredded cheese.

This is a good way to encourage picky eaters to try foods they might not usually touch.

nyiahsandisfunsuppliesss

ORGANIC

LIKE BUTTER BABY ORGANIC EDGE CONTROL T.M.

100% PURE HONEY

FRESH PRODUCT   350 ml

How to Make Your Own Edge Control

1. ½ cup of DIY flaxseed gel.
2. 2 tablespoons of avocado oil.
3. 2 tablespoons of raw honey.
4. 2 tablespoons of Jamaican castor oil.
5. 2 tablespoons of beeswax.
6. 1 teaspoon of vegetable glycerin.
7. 15 drops of lavender oil.
8. A small pot.

0 0045 8627 48242

Once you've made your flaxseed gel (which basically consists of boiling distilled water and flaxseeds together), pull out a glass bowl and put the gel, avocado oil, honey, castor oil, and vegetable glycerin into it. With your whisk (you can also use a blender, but I personally think it's easier with a whisk), mix all of the ingredients together. put in refrigerator for five days!

Best Before: 23/02/2025

One Little Shoe coloring and activity story

SMILES N FROWNS ™

I am important and you are two , we are sister let's stick together and take over the world and do what we do!

By: Destini Townsell